Wooden Teeth & JELLY BEANS

Ray Nelson ★ Douglas Kelly ★ Ben Adams
Mike McLane ★ Thad Hendrickson

Ranjy Thomas: Executive Producer on Project Prezquest

In cooperation with Pete Smith and Keith Melder of the
National Museum of American History, Smithsonian Institution

SCHOLASTIC INC.
New York Toronto London Auckland
Sydney Mexico City New Delhi Hong Kong

ISBN 978-0-545-16643-0

13 12 11 10 9 8 7   11 12 13 14 15/0

Printed in the U.S.A.   40

First Scholastic printing, February 2009

PREZQUEST.COM

**YOUR FAMILY
YOUR POLITICS
YOUR PRESIDENT**

The buck may stop here, but the learning doesn't!

Go to *www.prezquest.com* to learn more about U.S. Presidents through:

- *Activities for parents and kids*
- *FREE classroom materials*
- *Fun & educational cartoons*
- *Interactive games*

Your Secret Code

EAGLE

Go to www.prezquest.com and type in your secret word: Eagle

PrezQuest

US PRESIDENTS

- Games
- Print Materials
- Cartoons
- Live Event
- Teacher Lessons
- Tell a Friend

JOIN FRABOOM

UP NEXT

PREZQUEST

NEXT CLASS STARTS IN:

2:03

fraboom
network

www.prezquest.com

Visit the website now & sign up for your guided presidential adventure.

Online live events are an exciting new technology that bring parents and children together through education and fun! These half-hour sessions are run by a live teacher who appears by webcam and refers to each individual student by name. You'll play games with kids from around the country, hear some of America's greatest presidents share their stories and learn all kinds of fun new facts about the U.S. Presidency. Sign up for your online live event today on PrezQuest.com!

Log on
to learn more!

Look for this icon in the book...

If you find this icon, it means that you can learn more about a certain topic by visiting www.prezquest.com. Enter the number on the icon into the "topic number box" on the PrezQuest.com home page and more fun content about the chosen topic will pop up onto the screen.

PREZQUEST
7 .COM

fraboom
network

WHAT TO EXPECT
• Guided Event with a Live Presenter
• Fun & Educational Cartoons
• 30-Minute Experience
• Interactive Games
• Printable Activity Book

SOME WORDS YOU'LL NEED TO KNOW

Ambassador — A person appointed to represent his or her government in its relations with other governments.

Assassination — The murder of a famous person.

Cabinet — A group of people picked by the president to run different departments and to act as advisors.

Congress — The top law-making group in the United States. It consists of the Senate and the House of Representatives.

Constitution — The document that sets forth the system of basic laws and beliefs that guide the functions and the limits of the government in running the country.

Continental Congress — The group of individuals that ran the United States during the revolutionary times (1774 to 1789). This group was organized to voice concerns against Great Britain, to organize the Continental Army, and to serve as the executive and law-making arms of the government.

Declaration of Independence — The proclamation by the Continental Congress declaring the 13 American colonies politically independent from Great Britain.

Impeachment — To charge the president with wrongdoing in office before a proper court of justice. This is the first step in removing a president from office.
(See presidents John Tyler, Andrew Johnson, Richard Nixon and Bill Clinton.)

Inauguration or inaugural — To enter into the office of president with a formal ceremony and/or celebration.

Secede — To formally withdraw from a membership or alliance.

Veto — The power under the Constitution that the president has to reject a bill that has been passed by Congress.

I was once honored to be President of the United States of America. I had the privilege to sit in the same Oval Office and walk the same White House halls as Abraham Lincoln, Teddy Roosevelt, and John F. Kennedy. We all got there through persistence, hard work and, most importantly, education.

Within this book, you will learn about the lives of each president and what he faced while holding our nation's highest office. You will see that every president has at least one thing in common with you—each was a human being. They enjoyed hobbies, pets, and friends and worked at other jobs before becoming president. Not every student will become president, but everyone *can* become president.

For me, being President of the United States was both an honor and fun. This will be true for the dream you choose to pursue. Begin now by building your greatest asset—an education.

Gerald R. Ford

Gerald R. Ford

Leaves began falling and the weather turned cool. An **election** was brewing in Rhino Grade School.

The best and the brightest are running this year, to lead Rhino School to the future frontier. Whom will they choose? What will they do? They'll all have to **vote** for one of these two.

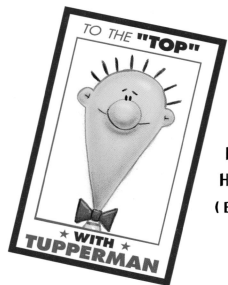

TO THE "TOP" WITH ★ TUPPERMAN ★

Tommy **T**upperman is quiet and shy. He's a little bit boring, he's just a bit dry. (OK, here's the real truth.) He has lifeless hair, his clothes are all blah. His overall dullness will leave you in awe. (But other than that, he's a really nice kid!)

Penelope **R**atsworth is one of the two. If she doesn't beat Tommy, she might beat on you. She has a slight temper and sometimes she's **rude.** She acts like a pit bull in a bad **mood.** She's quick with a promise, she goes with the **flow,** And if you don't vote for her, she'll step on your **toe.**

VOTE FOR RATSWORTH

When the polls came out,
Tommy said with a sigh,
"I'm getting lambasted —
why do I try ❓

I stick by my morals,
I try not to bend,
but my rating is
lower than an
earthworm's rear end!

People don't like me,
not one little bit.
Maybe, just maybe,
it's best if I quit."

I would vote for you, Tommy!

Our hero **Tommy** was filled with despair,
When he came eye to eye with a powerful glare.
George looked at **Tommy**, and he seemed to say,

"I cannot believe that you're acting this way!"

Tommy began feeling
a small bit of shame,
He realized that quitting
wasn't part of this game.

There's an election to win,
there's no time to rest.
We must get to work,
we can learn from the best.

THE TUPPERMAN FILES

PRESIDENTS

HOW IS A PRESIDENT ELECTED?

Every four years, the United States chooses someone to be president and someone to be vice president. This election process is done in two steps: a primary election and a general election.

In the primary election, candidates for president compete for the nomination of their political party, such as the Democratic, Republican, and Libertarian parties. Each candidate gets committed delegates (which are like points) based on the number of votes they get in each state. The date of the primary election may be different from state to state. During the summer of an election year, each political party holds a convention and adds up the delegates for each person running for president. The candidate with over half the total delegates gets the nomination of his or her party. The winner then chooses someone to run as vice president on the "ticket."

In the general election, the winners of the primary election face off against each other. Sometimes independent candidates (people without a political party) join in the race too. The general election is always held in early November. When all the votes are added up at the end of election day, the candidate with the most votes in a state wins all the delegates (called electoral votes) in that state. (These delegates form what is called the Electoral College.) The number of electoral votes for each state is equal to the number of the state's members in Congress—two senators plus the representatives. There are 538 total electoral votes in the 50 states and the District of Columbia. The candidate who gets 270 or more electoral votes wins the presidency! (Think about this: It is possible to win the electoral vote and the presidency but come in second in the total number of votes by citizens, called the "popular vote.")

Learn more about the Electoral College at www.prezquest.com

PREZQUEST
17
.COM

GEORGE WASHINGTON

February 22, 1732 (Fredericksburg, Virginia) **Born**
December 14, 1799 **Died**
No party (first term); Federalist (second term) **Party**
John Adams **Vice presidents**
6 feet 2 inches tall, 175 pounds **Physical**
WIFE "Lady" Martha Custis SON John DAUGHTER Martha **Family**
[both adopted by Washington]

✪ PERSONAL ✪

Washington liked to play billiards and cards. He also enjoyed reading newspapers and taking daily walks.

★ I Have a Splinter in My Tongue—Not!

No! George Washington *did not* own a pair of false teeth made out of wood. He did wear false teeth, but his first pair were made of hippopotamus ivory. He also had teeth made of lead, ivory, and the teeth of humans, sheep, and cows.

✪ PRESIDENTIAL FIRSTS ✪

First president to be younger than his wife

★ First to have his picture on a postage stamp

★ Favorite Foods

Crabmeat soup and egg nog

★ I Cannot Tell a Lie—I Lied

George Washington never said, "I cannot tell a lie, 'twas I cut down the cherry tree." This story, along with some other tall tales, came from a book written in 1800 called *The Life of George Washington; With Curious Anecdotes, Equally Honorable to Himself and Exemplary to His Young Countrymen.*

★ What Happened?

1789 - First official Thanksgiving
1789 - First Postmaster General: Timothy Pickering
1791 - First U.S. Mint (where money is made)
1791 - First U.S. Census

★ Crossing the Delaware

As the commander of the Continental Army, General Washington once led troops across an ice-filled Delaware River to win an important battle.

JOHN ADAMS

Born October 30, 1735 (Braintree [now Quincy], Massachusetts)
Died July 4, 1826 (the same day Thomas Jefferson died)
Party Federalist
Vice president Thomas Jefferson
Physical 5 feet 7 inches tall, 190 pounds
Family WIFE Abigail Smith SONS John Quincy, Charles, and Thomas DAUGHTER Abigail ("Nabby")

✪ PERSONAL ✪

Adams loved to take walks, go fishing, and read. He was always looking for new books to add to his personal library. Abigail Adams used to hang laundry to dry in the East Room of the White House.

✪ PRESIDENTIAL FIRSTS ✪

First vice president elected to the presidency

★

First to live in the White House

★

First president whose son would later become president

★

I Told You We Should've Asked for Directions!

While going to Washington, D.C., to move into the White House, John Adams and his family got lost for several hours in the woods north of the city.

★

Dot the i's and Cross the t's

After Thomas Jefferson finished writing the Declaration of Independence, John Adams had the task of revising it.

THOMAS JEFFERSON

April 13, 1743 (Goochland [now Albemarle] County, Virginia) Born
July 4, 1826 (the same day John Adams died) Died
Democratic-Republican Party
Aaron Burr (1801-1805) and George Clinton (1805-1812) Vice presidents
6 feet 2 inches tall Physical
WIFE Martha Skelton DAUGHTERS Martha ("Patsy") and Mary ("Polly") Family

✪ PRESIDENTIAL FIRSTS ✪

First president to be inaugurated in Washington, D.C.

★ What Has Hundreds of Legs and Flies?

During the signing of the Declaration of Independence, which Jefferson wrote, the ceremony ended early because of all the flies that were bothering the members. Jefferson liked to say that it was under the "influence of flies" that the Declaration of Independence was voted upon.

✪ PERSONAL ✪

Jefferson was a well-educated man who spoke six languages. He was an architect, lawyer, musician, and inventor. He spent many long hours working to pass laws guaranteeing freedom of religion.

★ Nice Duds!

Thomas Jefferson liked to dress in his farmer clothes.

★ Friends 'Til the End

Thomas Jefferson and John Adams became very good friends after being president and wrote many letters to each other. They died on the same day, July 4, 1826, the 50th anniversary of the Declaration of Independence.

JAMES MADISON

Born March 16, 1751 (Port Conway, Virginia)
Died June 28, 1836
Party Democratic-Republican
Vice presidents George Clinton (1809-1812) and Elbridge Gerry (1813-1814)
Physical 5 feet 4 inches tall, 100 pounds
Family WIFE Dorothea ("Dolley") Payne Todd ("The Toast of Washington")

★ The Hostess with the Mostest

Dolley Madison was the official White House hostess for sixteen years for James Madison and Thomas Jefferson. She refused to leave the White House during the British invasion in 1812, insisting on staying until she knew her husband and many of the White House treasures were safe. In 1814, the Capitol and the "Executive Mansion" were burned by the British. The outside of the mansion was painted white, which is why it is known as the "White House."

✪ PERSONAL ✪

Madison played chess, rode horseback, and liked to read old Latin and Greek books.

★ Author, Author

James Madison is known as the "Father of the Constitution"—a name he hated. He was the main author of the Constitution and served as secretary of the conference that drafted it.

✪ PRESIDENTIAL FIRSTS ✪

First president to be younger than both his vice presidents and to have both vice presidents die while in office

★

First to lead troops and to face enemy fire while in office

★

First to wear long pants—the previous presidents wore knickers (very short pants)

JAMES MONROE

April 28, 1758 (Westmoreland County, Virginia) Born
July 4, 1831 Died
Democratic-Republican Party
Daniel Tompkins Vice president
A little over 6 feet tall Physical
WIFE Elizabeth Kortright DAUGHTERS Eliza and Maria Hester Family

PRESIDENT
★5★
1817-1825

✪ PRESIDENTIAL FIRSTS ✪

**Only president to serve in two different cabinet posts
(secretary of state and secretary of war)**

★

First president to tour the country

✪ PERSONAL ✪

Monroe was a friendly and
polite person. He loved to ride
horses and go hunting.

★

The Monroe Doctrine

President Monroe was worried
that foreign countries like
Spain and Russia would take
over areas that were important to the
United States. He warned other countries
against expansion in the Western half
of the world. This message came
to be called the Monroe Doctrine.

JOHN QUINCY ADAMS

Born July 11, 1767 (Braintree [now Quincy], Massachusetts)
Died February 23, 1848
Party Democratic-Republican
Vice president John C. Calhoun
Physical 5 feet 7 inches tall, 175 pounds
Family WIFE Louisa Catherine Johnson SONS George, John II, and Charles
FATHER John Adams (the second president)

✪ PERSONAL ✪

Adams woke up every morning at 5 a.m., built a fire,
read the Bible, and bathed in the Potomac River.
He enjoyed reading, nature, horseback riding,
swimming, and going to the theater.

★
Skinny-Dipping

When John Quincy
Adams was president
he would take a
morning walk down to
the Potomac River and
swim naked. One
morning, a woman
news reporter named
Anne Royall sat on his
clothes until he gave
her an interview. He
did the interview while
standing chest deep in
the Potomac.

✪ PRESIDENTIAL FIRSTS ✪

First son of a president to become a president
★
First to have his photograph taken (1843)
★
Installed the first pool table in the White House

★
Man About the House

Adams is the only president
to be elected to the House
of Representatives after
his term as president.
(He served 17 years.)

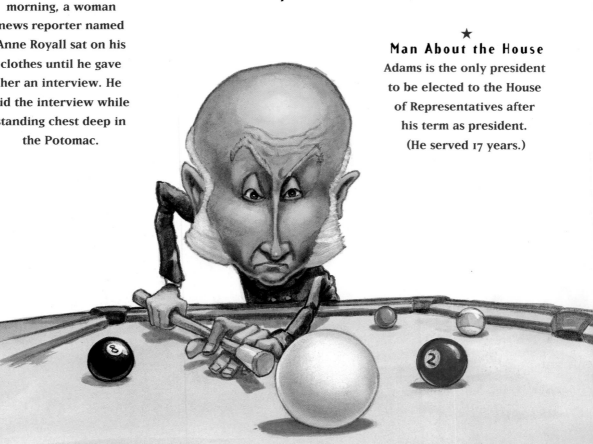

ANDREW JACKSON

March 15, 1767 (Waxhaw region between North and South Carolina) Born
June 8, 1845 Died
Democratic Party
John C. Calhoun (1829-1832), Martin Van Buren (1833-1837) Vice presidents
6 feet 1 inch tall, 145 pounds Physical
WIFE Rachel Donelson Robards SON Andrew Jr. [adopted nephew] Family

PRESIDENT

7

1829-1837

✪ PRESIDENTIAL FIRSTS ✪

First to survive an assassination attempt

★

Only president to help Congress pay off the national debt

★

Party Time

At Jackson's inaugural celebration, thousands of his supporters crashed the party at the White House. The farmers, woodsmen, and old soldiers tipped over tables, broke dishes, and climbed on furniture. To get rid of the crowd, waiters put giant tubs of punch on the White House lawn, luring people outside, and quickly locked the doors behind them.

✪ PERSONAL ✪

Jackson was orphaned at 14 years of age. He was adopted by uneducated, hard-working parents. He was nicknamed "Old Hickory."

★

Mr. Veto

Jackson vetoed more bills than all the presidents before him combined.

★

Take That!

On January 30, 1835, Richard Lawrence tried to assassinate Andrew Jackson. Both of Lawrence's guns misfired. Jackson chased after Lawrence, hitting him with his cane.

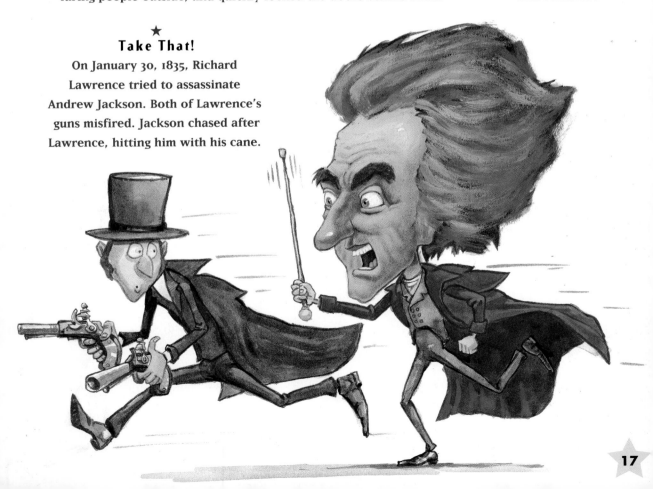

MARTIN VAN BUREN

Born December 5, 1782 (Kinderhook, New York)
Died July 24, 1862
Party Democratic
Vice president Richard Mentor Johnson
Physical 5 feet 5 inches tall
Family WIFE Hannah Hoes SONS Abraham, John, Martin Jr., and Smith

★ **Kissing Babies**

Martin Van Buren was the country's first true politician president. He used speeches, rallies, sing-alongs, leaflets, and fund-raisers. He was known as the "Little Magician," because everything he touched turned into votes.

✪ PRESIDENTIAL FIRSTS ✪

First president born as a citizen of the United States: **all the previous presidents were born before the Declaration of Independence, so they were born as British subjects.**

Learn more about the qualifications you must meet to become president at www.prezquest.com.

★ **I'm O.K., You're O.K.**

Van Buren's nickname was Old Kinderhook. He approved things by signing "O.K." Many believe that is where the phrase "O.K." came from.

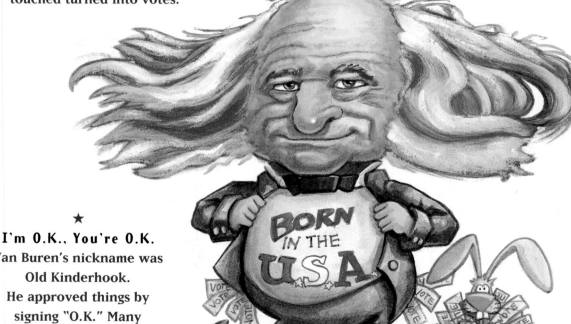

✪ PERSONAL ✪

Van Buren enjoyed attending the theater and the opera and going fishing.

WILLIAM HENRY HARRISON

February 9, 1773 (Charles City County, Virginia) **Born**

April 4, 1841 *Died*

Whig *Party*

John Tyler *Vice president*

5 feet 8 inches tall *Physical*

WIFE **Anna Tuthill Symmes** SONS **John Cleves, William, John Scott, Benjamin,** *Family* **and Carter** DAUGHTERS **Elizabeth, Lucy, Mary, and Anna**

PRESIDENT
9
1841

✪ PERSONAL ✪

Harrison was 68 when he was inaugurated. He enjoyed walking, horseback riding, and reading the Bible.

★ Pets

"His Whiskers" was Harrison's goat.

★ Bundle Up

William Henry Harrison gave the longest **inaugural** speech in history, lasting over one hour and 40 minutes. Harrison stood in a freezing cold March day without gloves, hat, or coat. He caught a terrible cold, which turned to pneumonia and killed him on April 4, 1841. He was president for only one month—the shortest term of any president.

✪ PRESIDENTIAL FIRSTS ✪

First president to die in office

JOHN TYLER

Born March 29, 1790 (Charles City County, Virginia)
Died January 18, 1862
Party Whig
Vice president None
Physical 6 feet tall; very thin build
Family WIVES Letitia Christian [died 1842], Julia Gardiner ("The Rose of Long Island") SONS Tazewell, John, Robert, David, John Alexander, Lachlan, Robert Fitzgerald, and Lyon DAUGHTERS Alice, Letitia, Elizabeth, Mary, Anne, Julia, and Pearl

✪ PRESIDENTIAL FIRSTS ✪
First president to have no vice president during an entire term

★ Pets
Tyler had a horse named "General," a pet canary named "Johnny Ty," and an Italian greyhound named "Le Beau."

★ Think of the Diapers
John Tyler had more children than any other president—a grand total of 15.

✪ PERSONAL ✪
Tyler hunted fox and loved wild animals. Tyler and his wife, Julia, had some of the greatest parties ever given in the White House. Tyler would play his violin accompanied by Julia on the guitar.

★ Too Many Vetoes?
In 1841, impeachment proceedings were started against Tyler for misusing his veto power.

JAMES KNOX POLK

November 2, 1795 (Mecklenburg County, North Carolina) **Born**
June 15, 1849 **Died**
Democratic Party
George Mifflin Dallas Vice president
5 feet 8 inches tall Physical
WIFE **Sarah Childress** Family

★
I'll Buy Boardwalk
James Polk was known as the "real estate" president. During his term, the United States added 800,000 square miles of territory. He settled a boundary dispute with the British over the Oregon Territory. He also had the United States fight a war with Mexico to take the area in the Southwest that included New Mexico, Texas, and California.

❂ PRESIDENTIAL FIRSTS ❂
First president to voluntarily retire after one term

★
It's My Party...
James Polk wasn't a popular president. He and Mrs. Polk had some of the most boring parties ever to be thrown in the White House. Dancing and music were no-nos.

ZACHARY TAYLOR

Born November 24, 1784 (Orange County, Virginia)
Died July 9, 1850
Party Whig
Vice president Millard Fillmore
Physical 5 feet 8 inches tall, 170 pounds
Family WIFE Margaret ("Peggy") Mackall Smith SON Richard
DAUGHTERS Ann, Sarah, and Mary

✪ PRESIDENTIAL FIRSTS ✪

First president who never held a political office before the presidency

★

First to be elected from a state west of the Mississippi River (Louisiana)

★

Hey, Pal! Buy Yourself a Postcard

Taylor's faithful old war-horse, "Whitey," was allowed to graze on the White House front lawn. Some people say that tourists actually pulled hairs from Whitey's tail as souvenirs.

★

Old Rough and Ready

Before becoming president, Taylor was a general in the Army.

✪ PERSONAL ✪

Taylor was a very warm and personable man, although at times he was a little bit shy. He chewed tobacco and was famous for never missing a spittoon when he spat.

★

Seconds, Anyone?

Taylor spent an entire day at the Fourth of July ceremony laying the cornerstone of the Washington Monument. The day was scorching hot, and when the president got home, he ate giant helpings of cherries, iced milk, and pickled cucumbers, all while suffering from a case of typhus fever. He became quite ill and died five days later on July 9, 1850.

MILLARD FILLMORE

January 7, 1800 (Locke Township, Cayuga County, New York) Born
March 8, 1874 Died
Whig Party
None Vice president
6 feet tall Physical
WIFE Abigail Powers SON Millard DAUGHTER Mary Family

★ Book Him, Dano!

Millard Fillmore didn't go to school when he was a child, so he didn't know many words and could barely read. He visited a library in his town and discovered a whole new world. He enrolled at an academy in New Hope, New York, where he met and eventually married teacher Abigail Powers. During his presidency, Millard and Abigail started the first permanent library in the White House. They had a personal library of over 4,000 books.

✪ PERSONAL ✪

Fillmore enjoyed collecting books. He was nicknamed "Last of the Whigs."

✪ PRESIDENTIAL FIRSTS ✪

First president to have a stepmother
★
His wife, Abigail, had the first bathtub with running water installed in the White House.

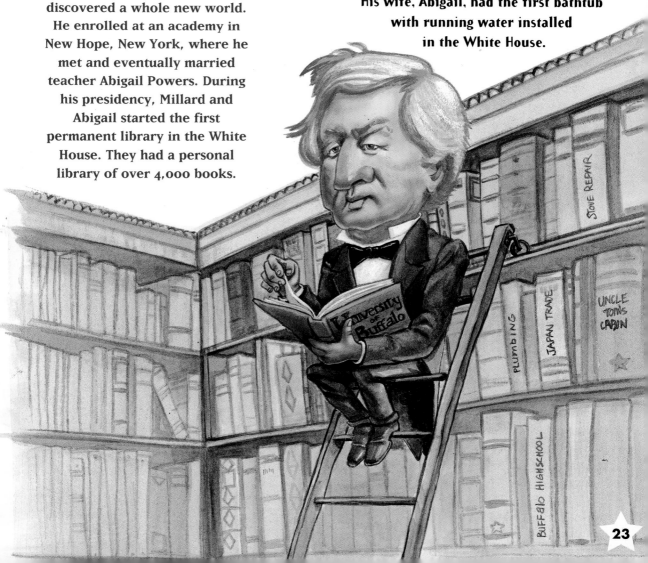

FRANKLIN PIERCE

Born November 23, 1804 (Hillsborough, New Hampshire)
Died October 8, 1869
Party Democratic
Vice president William Rufus DeVane King
Physical 5 feet 10 inches tall
Family WIFE Jane Means Appleton SONS Franklin [died when three days old], Frank Robert [died when four years old], and Benjamin [died in an accident two months before the inauguration]

✪ PRESIDENTIAL FIRSTS ✪

First president whose vice president never served, because he died before assuming any responsibilities

★

Only president to retain his original cabinet during his four years as president

★

First to put a Christmas tree in the White House

★

Kansas-Nebraska Act

The Kansas-Nebraska Act was strongly supported by Pierce. The Act let settlers in the Nebraska and Kansas territories decide for themselves whether to make slavery legal. People from the slave-state of Missouri illegally poured over the Kansas borders to vote in favor of slavery. The battles that took place because of the conflict generated the name "Bleeding Kansas." Opponents of the Act met in Wisconsin and started a new political force called the Republican Party.

✪ PERSONAL ✪

Pierce was an understanding person who made friends quite easily. He did, however, suffer from periods of depression and had a longtime battle with alcoholism. Pierce was an avid fisherman.

JAMES BUCHANAN

April 23, 1791 (Mercersburg, Pennsylvania) **Born**
June 1, 1868 *Died*
Democratic *Party*
John Cabell Breckinridge *Vice president*
6 feet tall *Physical*
Buchanan was never married. Harriet Lane, his niece, served as hostess. *Family*

PRESIDENT
15
1857-1861

✪ PERSONAL ✪

Buchanan enjoyed reading, playing cards, and entertaining his friends. When he talked to people he tipped his head to the left and closed one eye because one of his eyes was farsighted while the other was nearsighted. To make the matter worse, his left eye sat a bit higher in the socket.

✪ PRESIDENTIAL FIRSTS ✪

First president to send a transatlantic telegram: on August 16, 1858, he exchanged greetings with Queen Victoria of Great Britain.

★
Good Riddance

Buchanan sent a note to newly elected President Abraham Lincoln stating, "My Dear Sir: If you are as happy on entering the White House as I on leaving, you are a happy man indeed."

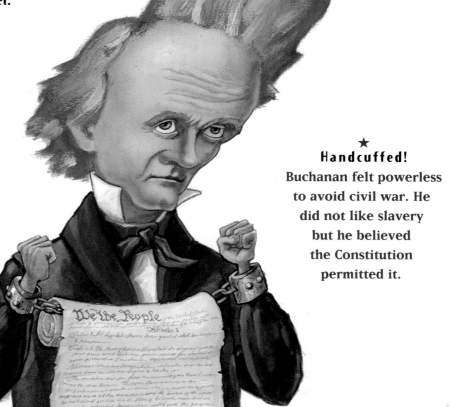

★
Handcuffed!

Buchanan felt powerless to avoid civil war. He did not like slavery but he believed the Constitution permitted it.

★
Spy vs. Spy
Lincoln's wife, Mary, had four brothers and four brothers-in-law who fought for the South during the Civil War. There were many rumors throughout Washington, D.C., that Mary Lincoln was a Confederate spy. Abe was so distressed by these rumors that he appeared personally at a Senate hearing to denounce them.

★
Favorite Food
Fricasseed chicken

PREZQUEST 16 .COM

To watch a cartoon about Lincoln, go to www.prezquest.com and enter the number 16 in the topic box.

★
Nickname
Honest Abe

L I N C O L N

February 12, 1809 (Hodgenville, Hardin [now Larue] County, Kentucky) **Born**
April 15, 1865 **Died**
Republican **Party**
Hannibal Hamlin (1861-1865) and Andrew Johnson (1865) **Vice presidents**
6 feet 4 inches tall (he was the tallest president), 180 pounds **Physical**
WIFE Mary Todd SONS Robert, William ("Willie"), and Thomas ("Tad") **Family**

PRESIDENT
16
1861–1865

✪ PRESIDENTIAL FIRSTS✪

First president to be photographed at his inauguration (his second, in 1865).
In the photo, John Wilkes Booth can be seen standing close to Lincoln.
(John Wilkes Booth assassinated Lincoln in 1865.)

✪ PERSONAL ✪

Lincoln liked to read, go to the theater, play chess,
and share stories and jokes with his friends.
He also spent a good many hours splitting wood.
He was a man of great character and suffered a great
deal personally to keep the United States united.

★ Did'ya Hear the One About the...

Abraham Lincoln loved to tell jokes, poems, and stories. He was quite famous during his time for replying to questions with "That reminds me of a story." Lincoln laughed and joked about politics, the Civil War, and even himself. Lincoln was not considered very good-looking. When Senator Stephen Douglas called him a "two-faced man," Lincoln replied: "I leave it to my audience. If I had another face, do you think I would wear this one?"

★ What Happened?

1861—1865 - Civil War
1861 - Virginia, Arkansas, Alabama, Florida, Georgia, Louisiana, Mississippi, South Carolina, Texas, Tennessee, and North Carolina secede from the U.S. to form the Confederate States of America.
1863 - Emancipation Proclamation - Lincoln frees the slaves
1863 - Gettysburg Address
1865 - Confederate General Robert E. Lee surrenders at Appomattox Courthouse.
1865 - Lincoln assassinated by John Wilkes Booth.

★ Pets

"Bob," a gray and white Maltese cat; "Jack," the Lincoln family's pet turkey,
who was saved by the Lincoln boys from Thanksgiving dinner;
and "Jib," a mongrel dog who would often sit on Abe's lap and eat table scraps.

ANDREW JOHNSON

Born December 29, 1808 (Raleigh, North Carolina)
Died July 31, 1875
Party Democratic
Vice president None
Physical 5 feet 10 inches tall
Family WIFE Eliza McCardle SONS Charles, Robert, and Andrew DAUGHTERS Martha and Mary

★ Have I Got a Deal for You!

In 1867, the United States bought the Alaska Territory from Russia for $7.2 million. The people living in Alaska were given three years to decide whether they wanted to stay in Alaska or move back to Russia.

✪ PRESIDENTIAL FIRSTS ✪

First president to be impeached

★

First visit by a queen — Queen Emma, of the Sandwich Islands (Hawaii) — to an American president, on August 14, 1866

✪ PERSONAL ✪

Johnson was a great speaker. He liked the circus and minstrel shows, vegetable gardening, and playing checkers.

★ A Stitch in Time

When Andrew Johnson was 14, he and his brother were sold as servants to a tailor. The boys had to work for the tailor, who in turn gave them food, clothing, and shelter, and taught them how to be tailors. After two years the boys ran away. The tailor ran an ad offering a $10 reward for their return, but the boys were never caught.

ULYSSES SIMPSON GRANT

April 27, 1822 (Point Pleasant, Ohio) Born
July 23, 1885 Died
Republican Party
Schuyler Colfax (1869–1873) and Henry Wilson (1873–1875) Vice presidents
5 feet 7 inches tall Physical
WIFE Julia Boggs Dent SONS Frederick, Ulysses ("Buck"), and Jesse Family
DAUGHTER Ellen ("Nellie")

PRESIDENT
18
1869–1877

★

License and Registration, Please

Grant was riding his racing horse one day in downtown Washington, D.C., when a police officer gave him a ticket for speeding. The officer didn't recognize the president and fined him $20. The president paid his $20 fine and sent a commendation to the officer.

✪ PRESIDENTIAL FIRSTS ✪

First president to have both parents alive when taking office

★

**First presidential candidate to have a female opponent
(Victoria Claflin Woodhull)**

✪ PERSONAL ✪

Grant was a West Point graduate and the commanding general of the Union Army at the end of the Civil War. He liked to smoke cigars, race horses, draw, and paint.

★ The Name Game

Grant's original name was Hiram Ulysses Grant. When he was accepted to West Point, he didn't want the initials H.U.G. labeled on his possessions, so he switched his name to Ulysses Hiram Grant. When he got to school, he found he was registered by the name Ulysses Simpson Grant. He liked the name and kept it.

★ Favorite Breakfast
Cucumbers soaked in vinegar

RUTHERFORD BIRCHARD HAYES

Born October 4, 1822 (Delaware, Ohio)
Died January 17, 1893
Party Republican
Vice president William Almon Wheeler
Physical 5 feet 7 inches tall, 175 pounds
Family WIFE Lucy Ware Webb SONS Sardis, James, Rutherford Platt, and Scott
DAUGHTER Frances ("Fanny")

✪ PERSONAL ✪

Hayes was serious, honest, and hardworking.
He enjoyed the outdoors, reading, playing chess, and landscaping his home grounds.

✪ PRESIDENTIAL FIRSTS ✪

First president to use the telephone

★

First to visit the West Coast while in office

★

First president elected after losing the popular vote
(see how a president is elected on page 54)

★ Hey, Kid! Get Off My Lawn

First Lady Lucy Hayes started the traditional annual Easter Egg Roll at the White House. The event had been held on the Capitol lawn, but Congress complained that the event ruined the grass.

★ Thirsty?

"Lemonade Lucy" was the nickname given to Lucy Hayes because she wouldn't allow any alcohol to be served in the White House. She also didn't allow any smoking, dancing, or card playing.

JAMES ABRAM GARFIELD

November 19, 1831 (Orange, Cuyahoga County, Ohio) **Born**
September 19, 1881 **Died**
Republican **Party**
Chester Alan Arthur **Vice president**
6 feet tall, 185 pounds **Physical**
WIFE Lucretia ("Crete") Rudolph **SONS** Harry, James, Irvin, and Abram **Family**
DAUGHTER Mary

PRESIDENT
20
1881

★
Quit Horsing Around

When he was a boy, James Garfield worked on the Erie Canal. He led the horses that pulled the floatboat *Evening Star* on the bank of the river. He was dunked quite a few times before he finally got the horses to cooperate.

✪ PRESIDENTIAL FIRSTS ✪

First left-handed president

★

First to campaign in more than one language (English and Spanish)

✪ PERSONAL ✪

Garfield was a friendly person who liked to hug people or put his arm around whomever he was talking to. He enjoyed playing chess and billiards and could write with either hand.

★
Assassination

James Garfield was shot on July 2, 1881, in a Baltimore railroad station. Charles J. Guiteau had been stalking the president for weeks but had never had the nerve to shoot him until July 2. Guiteau used a .44 British Bulldog pistol because he thought "it would look nice in a museum someday." Garfield lived for 80 days after he was shot.

CHESTER ALAN ARTHUR

Born October 5, 1830 (North Fairfield, Vermont)
Died November 18, 1886
Party Republican
Vice president None
Physical 6 feet 2 inches tall, 220 pounds
Family WIFE Ellen ("Nell") Lewis Herndon SON Chester Jr. DAUGHTER Ellen ("Nell")

✪ PRESIDENTIAL FIRSTS ✪

**First president to have his citizenship questioned
(many people believed he was born in Canada)**

First to take the oath of office in his own home

Favorite Food
Mutton chops

This Is a Test–This Is Only a Test

During Chester Arthur's time as president, a change in the civil service (government jobs) took place. A test was now to be given to those people wanting government jobs. This would make sure that the jobs were given to the people most qualified instead of the people doing favors for the politicians in charge of giving the jobs.

✪ PERSONAL ✪

To lighten the mood of the country after the serious personality of President Hayes and the sadness over President Garfield's assassination, Arthur redecorated the White House and entertained the people of Washington, D.C. He was a romantic gentleman who liked to fish and hunt.

STEPHEN GROVER CLEVELAND

March 18, 1837 (Caldwell, New Jersey) Born
June 24, 1908 Died
Democratic Party
Thomas Andrews Hendricks Vice president
5 feet 11 inches tall, 250 pounds Physical
WIFE Frances Folsom SONS Richard and Francis Family
DAUGHTERS Ruth, Esther, and Marion

PRESIDENT
22
1885–1889

★
But How Many Home Runs Did She Hit?

Some people think that the Baby Ruth candy bar was named after Cleveland's first daughter, Ruth. During Cleveland's first term, Ruth would play on the White House front lawn. She had to stop playing out front because too many tourists would pick her up and pass her around.

✪ PERSONAL ✪

Cleveland was known as an honest and good man. He was also quick-tempered and blunt. His favorite sport was fishing. He also liked to play cards and eat German food.

★
Honesty Is the Best Policy

Cleveland was known for his honesty. When he came to Washington, D.C., he began cleaning up the corruption that had occurred before he was president. He reviewed the records of many government employees and fired them if there was evidence of wrongdoing.

✪ PRESIDENTIAL FIRSTS ✪

Only president elected to two nonconsecutive terms (1885–1889 and 1893–1897)

★
Only president to be married in the White House and first to have a child born there

BENJAMIN HARRISON

Born August 20, 1833 (North Bend, Ohio)
Died March 13, 1901
Party Republican
Vice president Levi Parsons Morton
Physical 5 feet 6 inches tall
Family WIVES Caroline Lavinia Scott [died 1892], Mary Lord Dimmick SON Russell Benjamin DAUGHTERS Mary Scott ("Mamie") and Elizabeth

✪ PRESIDENTIAL FIRSTS ✪
Only grandson of a president to be elected to the presidency

★ You Light Up My Life

In 1891, the Edison Electric company installed the first electricity in the White House. After Benjamin Harrison got an electrical shock, the family often refused to touch the light switches. Sometimes the Harrison family went to bed leaving on all the lights in the White House.

★ Sooner or Later

When the Oklahoma Territory was opened up for expansion, settlers would race from designated areas at set times to claim plots of free land for their families. Some people cheated and left before they were supposed to. The cheating settlers became known as "Sooners."

✪ PERSONAL ✪
Harrison was known as the "Human Iceberg" because he was stiff and formal when dealing with people. He was very smart and paid attention to details.

★ Following in Grandpa's Footsteps

Benjamin Harrison's grandfather was William Henry Harrison, the ninth president.

STEPHEN GROVER CLEVELAND

March 18, 1837 (Caldwell, New Jersey) **Born**
June 24, 1908 **Died**
Democratic **Party**
Adlai E. Stevenson **Vice president**
5 feet 11 inches tall, 250 pounds **Physical**
WIFE **Frances Folsom** SONS **Richard and Francis** **Family**
DAUGHTERS **Ruth, Esther, and Marion**

PRESIDENT
24
1893-1897

★ A Three-Hour Cruise, a Three-Hour Cruise

Grover Cleveland went sailing in July 1893 for what many people thought was a fishing trip on the private yacht *Oneida*. But the trip was not for fishing. Cleveland secretly had surgery for a cancerous growth in his mouth. The operation was so secret that nobody found out about it until 1917 when one of the doctors let the secret slip out.

★ Veto, Veto

During his two terms, Grover Cleveland used his veto power 584 times. This is the highest total of any president except Franklin Roosevelt.

Learn more about presidential veto power at www.prezquest.com.

★ PRESIDENTIAL FIRSTS ★

Only president elected to two nonconsecutive terms (1885-1889 and 1893-1897)

★ Burning the Midnight Oil

Grover Cleveland was known for working extremely hard. Many times he could be found working well into the early morning hours.

WILLIAM McKINLEY

PRESIDENT

25

1897-1901

Born January 29, 1843 (Niles, Ohio)
Died September 14, 1901
Party Republican
Vice presidents Garret Augustus Hobart (1897–1899) and Theodore Roosevelt (1901)
Physical 5 feet 7 inches tall, 190 to 200 pounds
Family WIFE Ida Saxton DAUGHTERS Katherine ("Katie") and Ida [both died as babies]

✪PRESIDENTIAL FIRSTS✪
First president to campaign by telephone

★ Aloha!
In 1898, William McKinley signed a joint congressional resolution annexing (annexing means to add or to join to something bigger) the Hawaiian Islands.

✪PERSONAL✪
McKinley was a cheerful and friendly man loved by almost everyone. He enjoyed the opera, the theater, and cribbage.

Greetings From HAWAII

★ Assassination
In 1901, William McKinley was shot by Leon Czolgosz after giving a speech in Buffalo, New York. He lived for eight days after being shot.

★ Tie a Purple Ribbon 'Round the Ol' Oak Tree
William McKinley's wife, Ida, couldn't stand the color yellow. She banned anything yellow from being in the White House. She even ordered the gardeners to pull up all the yellow flowers.

THEODORE ROOSEVELT

October 27, 1858 (New York, New York) Born
January 6, 1919 Died
Republican Party
Charles Warren Fairbanks (1905-1909) Vice president
5 feet 8 inches tall, 200 pounds Physical
WIVES Alice Hathaway Lee [died 1884], Edith Kermit Carow Family
SONS Theodore Jr., Kermit, Archibald Bulloch, and Quentin
DAUGHTERS Alice and Ethel Carow

PRESIDENT
26
1901-1909

✪ PERSONAL ✪

Roosevelt was one of the most colorful presidents in U.S. history. He rode horseback, hunted, and boxed (even as president!). He wrote books about politics, America, outdoor pastimes, wilderness, and great adventures. The "teddy bear" was named after him in 1903, and his favorite word was "Bully!"– which meant *great*.

★
Dig, Dig, Dig

Roosevelt began the construction of the Panama Canal, which cost $400 million and took 43,000 workers to complete. It was finished in 1914. It is the easiest and shortest route for ships to travel between the Atlantic and Pacific oceans.

✪ PRESIDENTIAL FIRSTS ✪

First president to win a Nobel Peace Prize (in 1906)

★

First to visit a foreign country while in office

★

First to ride in a car, to ride in a submarine, and to fly in a plane (on October 11, 1910, he flew for four minutes in a plane built by the Wright brothers).

WILLIAM HOWARD TAFT

Born September 15, 1857 (Cincinnati, Ohio)
Died March 8, 1930
Party Republican
Vice president James Schoolcraft Sherman
Physical 6 feet 2 inches tall, 300-350 pounds
Family WIFE Helen ("Nellie") Herron SONS Robert Alphonso and Charles Phelps
DAUGHTER Helen Herron

✪ PRESIDENTIAL FIRSTS ✪

First president of all 48 connecting states

★

First to serve on the U.S. Supreme Court

★

First to throw a ceremonial first pitch at a baseball game

★
But Honey, I Wanna Be a Judge

William Taft never really wanted to be president. He wanted to be Chief Justice of the U.S. Supreme Court. His wife, however, wanted to be first lady, and talked him into running for president. In 1921, Taft got his wish and became the Chief Justice.

★
Pets

The Tafts kept their Holstein cow, "Pauline Wayne," on the White House front lawn.

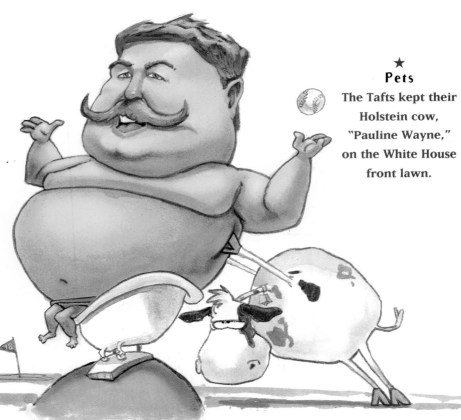

★
Big Bill

William Taft was the largest man ever to be president. Once he actually got stuck in a White House bathtub. After he was helped free, he ordered the installation of a special oversized bathtub, which could hold four normal-sized men.

✪ PERSONAL ✪

Taft was a very popular man with a cheerful personality and a wonderful sense of humor. He enjoyed playing golf and watching baseball. He was also a good dancer and tennis player.

THOMAS WOODROW WILSON

December 28, 1856 (Staunton, Virginia) **Born**
February 3, 1924 **Died**
Democratic **Party**
Thomas Riley Marshall **Vice president**
5 feet 11 inches tall **Physical**
WIVES **Ellen Louise Axson** [died 1914], **Edith Bolling Galt** Family
DAUGHTERS **Margaret Woodrow, Jessie Woodrow, and Eleanor Randolph**

✪ PERSONAL ✪

Wilson loved to attend the theater, especially vaudeville.

★ Not in Their League

One of Wilson's most important projects was the founding of the League of Nations. It was to be a large group of countries that would help settle arguments between countries to avoid wars. The U.S. Congress voted to not join the League of Nations. Without the United States, the League of Nations was never as powerful as planned.

★ Madame President

Toward the end of his presidency, Wilson suffered a stroke which paralyzed his left side. During his recovery, his wife, Edith, was his connection to the outside world. There probably hasn't been a more powerful first lady than Edith Wilson was during this time.

★ The War to End All Wars

World War I was fought from 1914 to 1918. The U.S. reluctantly joined the war against Germany in 1917 because German submarines would not stop sinking U.S. ships.

✪ PRESIDENTIAL FIRSTS ✪

First president to have earned a Ph.D.

★
First to cross the Atlantic while in office

★ Pets

Wilson had a sheep named "Old Ike" that chewed tobacco and grazed on the White House front lawn.

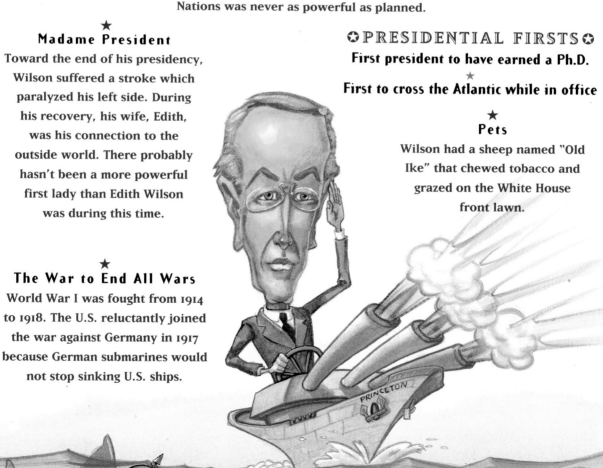

WARREN GAMALIEL HARDING

Born November 2, 1865 (Corsica, Ohio)
Died August 2, 1923
Party Republican
Vice president John Calvin Coolidge
Physical 6 feet tall
Family WIFE Florence Kling De Wolfe   DAUGHTER Elizabeth Ann Christian

✪ PRESIDENTIAL FIRSTS ✪

First president to visit Alaska

★

First to ride to his inauguration in a car

★

First to give a national speech over the radio

★ Hit Me!

Warren Harding would play poker at least twice a week. Once he gambled away an entire set of White House china dishes dating back to Benjamin Harrison. President Harding's political advisors were even given the nickname of the "Poker Cabinet."

★ We Can't All Be Perfect

During Harding's presidency, numerous scandals took place involving members of his staff. Secretary of the Interior Albert Fall, for example, sold for his own profit the country's oil reserves at Wyoming's Teapot Dome.

★ Pets

The Hardings had a canary named "Bob" and a dog named "Laddie Boy," which once had a birthday party in the White House.

★ Died in Office

Harding died of a heart attack while president.

OHIO GANG

✪ PERSONAL ✪

Harding tried to please other people and avoid confrontation.
He enjoyed playing golf and poker.

JOHN CALVIN COOLIDGE

July 4, 1872 (Plymouth, Vermont) **Born**
January 5, 1933 **Died**
Republican Party
Charles Gates Dawes (1925-1929) **Vice president**
5 feet 9 inches tall **Physical**
WIFE **Grace Anna Goodhue** SONS **John and Calvin** Family

PRESIDENT 30

1923-1929

Hey, Dad! Wake Up!

Vice president Coolidge was on vacation at his father's house when he learned that President Harding had died. At 2:47 a.m. on August 3, 1923, Coolidge was sworn into office by his father, John Coolidge, who was a justice of the peace. President Coolidge then went back to sleep.

★

Hi Ho, Nuts and Bolts! Away!

Coolidge had an electronic horse installed in the White House, and he would ride it almost every day.

✪ PERSONAL ✪

Calvin Coolidge enjoyed being photographed while wearing Indian headdresses and Boy Scout uniforms.

✪ PRESIDENTIAL FIRSTS ✪

First president to be sworn in by his father

★

First to have been born on the Fourth of July

★ Pets

The Coolidge family had dogs and cats, as well as a donkey named "Ebeneezer," a goose that had starred in a Broadway play, and a raccoon named "Rebecca." Occasionally, Coolidge was found walking around the White House with Rebecca on his shoulders.

41

HERBERT CLARK HOOVER

PRESIDENT

31

1929-1933

Born August 10, 1874 (West Branch, Iowa)
Died October 20, 1964
Party Republican
Vice president John Charles Curtis
Physical 5 feet 11 inches tall
Family WIFE Lou Henry SONS Herbert Jr. and Allan

✪ PRESIDENTIAL FIRSTS ✪

First president born west of the Mississippi River

⭐

Approved "The Star-Spangled Banner" as the national anthem

✪ PERSONAL ✪

Hoover was a hardworking man who was a bit shy and uncomfortable in crowds. He would exercise every morning by throwing a medicine ball around for 30 minutes.

⭐
Hey, Buddy, Can You Spare a Dime?

Herbert Hoover was president when the Great Depression took place. Hundreds of thousands of people lost their jobs and struggled to feed their families. Hoover was sad to see people cold and hungry, but he felt the government should not interfere with business. Even though it really wasn't his fault, Hoover was blamed for the Great Depression. Slums were called "Hoovervilles" and newspapers worn for warmth were called "Hoover blankets."

FRANKLIN DELANO ROOSEVELT

January 30, 1882 (Hyde Park, New York) Born
April 12, 1945 Died
Democratic Party
John Nance Garner (1933-41), Henry Agard Wallace (1941-45), Vice presidents
Harry S. Truman (1945)
6 feet 1 inch tall, 180 pounds Physical
WIFE Eleanor ("The First Lady of the World") Roosevelt (his fifth cousin) Family
SONS James, Elliott, Franklin Delano Jr., and John DAUGHTER Anna Eleanor

✪ PERSONAL ✪

Roosevelt contracted polio and became paralyzed in 1921. He swam to get his strength back. He wasn't sensitive about his disability, and often joked about it to make other people more comfortable.

★ A Day That Will Live in Infamy

On December 7, 1941, the Japanese bombed Pearl Harbor in Hawaii, killing 2,300 Americans and wounding 1,200 more. The next day, Roosevelt asked Congress for a declaration of war. With American support, the Allies (Great Britain, Canada, Russia, and France) were able to defeat the Axis powers (Germany Japan, and Italy) in 1945 to end World War II.

Fala

Major

PEARL HARBOR POOL

★ All in the Family

Franklin's fifth cousin was Theodore Roosevelt, the twenty-sixth president.

✪ PRESIDENTIAL FIRSTS ✪

First president whose mother was eligible to vote for him

★

First to be elected to more than two terms (he was elected four terms)

★

First to appear on television

★ It's a Dog Eat Dog Presidency

Roosevelt had a dog named "Fala" that was with him all the time. Reporters called Fala, "Fala the informer" because wherever the dog was, Roosevelt was not far behind. Roosevelt also had a German shepherd named "Major" that was famous for biting several politicians.

HARRY S. TRUMAN

Born May 8, 1884 (Lamar, Missouri)
Died December 26, 1972
Party Democratic
Vice president Alben William Barkley (1949-1953)
Physical 5 feet 10 inches tall, 185 pounds
Family WIFE Elizabeth ("Bess") Virginia Wallace DAUGHTER Margaret

✪ PRESIDENTIAL FIRSTS ✪
First president to give a speech on TV

★
OOPS!
On election day, 1948, the *Chicago Tribune* made a big mistake when it reported that Republican Thomas Dewey, not Truman, was the winner of the presidential election.

★
All Aboard!
During the 1948 presidential campaign, Harry Truman took a 30,000-mile whistle-stop tour of the United States. At each stop, many people would come to listen to Truman's speech. Many supporters would yell, "Give 'em hell, Harry!" The tour may have been the event that turned voters to Truman's favor.

★
The Buck Stops Here!
In his first six months as president, Truman brought an end to World War II, which included dropping two atomic bombs on Japan. He also prevented the expansion of communism and helped start the United Nations.

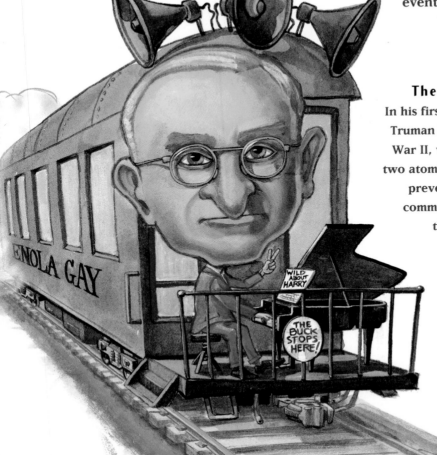

✪ PERSONAL ✪
Truman loved to play cards, horseshoes, and the piano.

DWIGHT DAVID EISENHOWER

October 14, 1890 (Denison, Texas) **Born**
March 28, 1969 **Died**
Republican **Party**
Richard M. Nixon **Vice president**
5 feet 10 inches tall, 178 pounds **Physical**
WIFE Mamie Geneva Doud **SON** John Sheldon **Family**

PRESIDENT
34
1953-1961

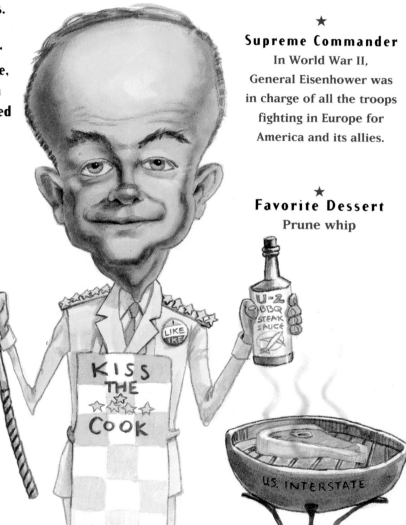

✪ PERSONAL ✪

Eisenhower was superstitious. He carried three coins in his pocket for good luck: a silver dollar, a five-guinea gold piece, and a French franc. He was a wonderful chef, who specialized in barbecued steaks. His nickname was "Ike."

★ Supreme Commander

In World War II, General Eisenhower was in charge of all the troops fighting in Europe for America and its allies.

★ Favorite Dessert
Prune whip

★ Bombs Away!

During Eisenhower's presidency, the United States started to build up gigantic numbers of nuclear missiles in the hopes that the Soviet Union would think twice before using its nuclear weapons against us.

✪ PRESIDENTIAL FIRSTS ✪

First president of all 50 states

★

First to appear on color television

★ Green With Envy

Eisenhower's favorite game was golf. He liked it so much that the United States Golf Association built a putting green near the White House so he could practice any time he wanted.

JOHN FITZGERALD KENNEDY

Born May 29, 1917 (Brookline, Massachusetts)
Died November 22, 1963
Party Democratic
Vice president Lyndon B. Johnson
Physical 6 feet tall, 170 pounds
Family WIFE Jacqueline Lee Bouvier SONS John Jr. and Patrick [died as a baby]
DAUGHTER Caroline

✪ PERSONAL ✪

President Kennedy thought his best quality was his curiosity and his worst was his irritability.
His charm, grace, and wit made him popular. He is remembered for the quotation,
"Ask not what your country can do for you, ask what you can do for your country."

★
One of These Days... Pow! Right to the Moon!

President Kennedy set a goal for the United States of putting a man on the moon
by the end of the decade. During Kennedy's term, the National Aeronautics and
Space Administration (NASA) started testing the effects of weightlessness in space
and of re-entry on human pilots. Astronauts Neil Armstrong and Buzz Aldrin
walked on the moon on July 20, 1969.

✪ PRESIDENTIAL FIRSTS ✪

**First to have won a Pulitzer Prize
(for the book *Profiles in Courage*)**

★
Assassination

John Kennedy was shot
by Lee Harvey Oswald on
November 22, 1963.

LYNDON BAINES JOHNSON

August 27, 1908 (Stonewall, Texas) **Born**
January 22, 1973 **Died**
Democratic **Party**
Hubert Horatio Humphrey (1965-1969) **Vice president**
6 feet 3 inches tall, 210 pounds **Physical**
WIFE **Claudia Alta ("Lady Bird") Taylor** DAUGHTERS **Lynda Bird and** Family
Luci Baines (All of the Johnsons had the initials "LBJ.")

✪ PRESIDENTIAL FIRSTS ✪

First president to have the oath of office administered by a woman

★

First to take the oath of office in an airplane

✪ PERSONAL ✪

Johnson was very competitive. One of his favorite activities was to take visitors on 90-mile-per-hour rides around his Texas ranch in his Lincoln Continental.

★
The Great Society

Johnson wanted to be remembered for turning America into the "Great Society"—a place without ignorance, poverty, and racial injustice. Unfortunately, Johnson is most remembered for the Vietnam War, which was so negative that he didn't run for re-election.

★
Pets

"Him" and "Her" were the Johnsons' pet beagles. Him's paw prints are imprinted in cement in the walkway leading to the White House press room. FBI director J. Edgar Hoover gave Johnson a beagle named "Edgar."

★
Favorite Foods

Canned green peas and tapioca

47

RICHARD MILHOUS NIXON

Born January 9, 1913 (Yorba Linda, California)
Died April 22, 1994
Party Republican
Vice presidents Spiro T. Agnew (1969-1973) and Gerald R. Ford (1973-1974)
Physical 5 feet 11 inches tall, 175 pounds
Family WIFE Thelma Catherine Patricia ("Pat") Ryan DAUGHTERS Patricia ("Tricia") and Julie

★ Watergate

Some of the people that Nixon hired to help him as president were found guilty of wrongdoings that came to be known as the "Watergate scandals." These wrongdoings included planting of listening devices in the Democratic office at the Watergate building. In 1974, impeachment proceedings began against President Nixon for covering up the Watergate scandals. When Nixon realized that he faced almost certain impeachment, he decided to resign.

★ Ping-Pong Diplomacy

In 1972, Richard Nixon took "A Journey for Peace." He traveled to China to meet with Chairman Mao Tse-Tung in hopes of broadening scientific, cultural, and trade contacts.

✪ PRESIDENTIAL FIRSTS ✪

First president to visit China while in office

✪ PERSONAL ✪

Nixon suffered from motion sickness and hay fever.

July 14, 1913 (Omaha, Nebraska) Born
December 26, 2006 Died
Republican Party
Nelson A. Rockefeller Vice president
6 feet tall, 195 pounds Physical
WIFE **Elizabeth Anne ("Betty") Bloomer Warren** SONS **Michael Gerald,** Family
John ("Jack"), and Steven Meigs DAUGHTER **Susan Elizabeth**

★ Helpful Hand

In an effort to bring an end
to a period of conflict
in America, Ford pardoned
former President Nixon for
Watergate and offered
clemency to draft dodgers
and deserters from the
Vietnam War.

✪ PRESIDENTIAL FIRSTS ✪

First to be appointed as vice president under the 25th
Amendment to the Constitution, when Spiro T. Agnew
resigned in 1973

★

Only president to serve without being chosen in
a national election

★ Good Sport

Gerald Ford was on the University of Michigan
football team from 1931 to 1934. In 1935, he played
in a college all-star game against the Chicago
Bears. He was offered tryouts by both the Green
Bay Packers and the Detroit Lions. While he was
in office, Ford continued to participate in
athletics, and enjoyed swimming, lifting weights,
skiing, and playing golf. In 1977, he had a
hole-in-one at the Memphis Classic.

✪ PERSONAL ✪

Ford was considered to be the most
athletic president to occupy the
White House. He was a right-handed
sportsman, yet he wrote and
ate with his left hand.

JAMES EARL CARTER

Born October 1, 1924 (Plains, Georgia)
Party Democratic
Vice president Walter Mondale
Physical 5 feet 9 inches tall, 155 pounds
Family WIFE Eleanor Rosalynn Smith SONS John, James, and Jeffrey DAUGHTER Amy

★
Favorite Foods
Mixed nuts
and peaches

✪ PERSONAL ✪
Carter studied nuclear physics at the Naval Academy.
He liked to wear denim "peanut clothes" and often wore
his "lucky" red tie.

★
A Little Light Reading
Jimmy Carter is a speed-reader. He has been
recorded reading 2,000 words a minute. It
was common for him to read two or three
books a week while he was president.

✪ PRESIDENTIAL FIRSTS ✪
First president to graduate from Annapolis
(the U.S. Naval Academy)

★
Creamy or Chunky
In 1953, Jimmy Carter returned from the Navy to Plains, Georgia, to take over the peanut farm
left by his late father. He improved production and expanded the scale of the farm so that it
became a thriving business. By 1979, he had become a millionaire in the peanut industry.

RONALD WILSON REAGAN

February 6, 1911 (Tampico, Illinois) **Born**
June 5, 2004 **DIED**
Republican **Party**
George Bush **Vice president**
6 feet 1 inch tall, 185 pounds **Physical**
WIVES **Jane Wyman [divorced 1948], Nancy Davis** **Family**
SONS **Michael and Ronald Jr.** DAUGHTERS **Maureen and Patti**

1981-1989

✪ PRESIDENTIAL FIRSTS ✪

Only president to have been divorced

★

First to be wounded by and to survive an assassination attempt

★

Only president to be inaugurated after his 70th birthday

★

Lights, Camera, Action

Reagan was a successful actor before he entered politics. He acted in such television shows and movies as *Knute Rockne, All American; Death Valley Days; Bedtime for Bonzo;* and a 1958 production called *A Turkey for President.*

★

Favorite Foods

Lasagna, macaroni and cheese, and jelly beans (his favorite jelly bean flavor was coconut)

✪ PERSONAL ✪

Reagan was known as the "Great Communicator" because he used television so well to present his policies and programs. He enjoyed working on his ranch in California clearing brush, building fences, and chopping wood.

GEORGE HERBERT WALKER BUSH

Born June 12, 1924 (Milton, Massachusetts)
Party Republican
Vice president James Danforth Quayle
Physical 6 feet 2 inches tall, 195 pounds
Family WIFE Barbara Pierce SONS George, John ("Jeb"), Neil, and Marvin
DAUGHTERS Dorothy ("Doro") and Robin [died of leukemia at age four]

★ Desert Storm

On August 2, 1990, Iraq invaded the country of Kuwait. Bush ordered operation Desert Shield—a series of diplomatic actions and embargoes. Desert Shield failed to work, so operation Desert Storm was started on January 17, 1991. Desert Storm involved massive bombing and ground attacks. American troops liberated Kuwait City, the capital of Kuwait. The war lasted until President Bush called for a cease-fire on February 27, 1991.

★ Tumbling Down

The Berlin Wall, a symbol of the Cold War erected in 1961, was taken down on November 9, 1989.

★ Eat Your Vegetables, George

Broccoli farmers were upset when George Bush said that he did not like broccoli. The farmers sent truckloads of broccoli to the White House. Barbara Bush graciously accepted the broccoli, but President Bush said, "I am President of the United States and I don't have to eat it."

✪ PERSONAL ✪

Bush is a quiet, gentle man who would much rather talk than fight. He played first base for the Yale baseball team.

WILLIAM JEFFERSON CLINTON

August 19, 1946 (Hope, Arkansas) Born
Democratic Party
Albert Gore Vice president
6 feet 1 inch tall, 200 pounds Physical
WIFE Hillary Rodham DAUGHTER Chelsea Family

✪ PRESIDENTIAL FIRSTS ✪

First president to have been a Rhodes scholar

✪ PERSONAL ✪

Clinton is the first "baby boomer" president. During his campaign he got a reputation for enjoying fast food and for being an avid jogger. In 1963, when Bill Clinton was 16 years old, he was a member of the Arkansas group to the Boy's Nation program. The highlight was a meeting at the White House with then-President John Kennedy.

★ Impeached!

President Clinton was impeached by the House of Representatives on December 19, 1998, and acquitted by the Senate on February 12, 1999.

★ Pet

"Socks" the cat

★ Favorite Foods

Mango Ice Cream
Peanut butter and banana

★ Sax Appeal

Bill Clinton plays both the tenor and the soprano saxophone. During his campaign, he made many appearances playing the saxophone, entertaining voters all across America.

GEORGE WALKER BUSH

Born July 6th, 1946 (New Haven, Connecticut)
Party Republican
Vice president Dick Cheney
Physical 5 feet 11 inches, 190 pounds
Family WIFE Laura Welch DAUGHTERS Barbara and Jenna, twins

✪ PERSONAL ✪

George W. Bush grew up in Texas. He left the state to attend Yale University and Harvard Business School. In 1975, he returned to Texas to go into the oil business. He married Laura Welch in 1977.

★

Like Father, Like Son

George W. Bush is the second president whose father was also president. His father, George Bush, was the 41st president.

★

Pets

One dog, Spot, and two cats, India and Ernie

★

Nickname

Dubya
(for his middle initial)

★

Play Ball

George W. Bush was managing general partner of the Texas Rangers baseball team before he became governor of Texas in 1994.

★

Close Race

George W. Bush is the third president to win the electoral vote without winning the popular vote. After one of the closest U.S. presidential elections in history, the American people waited for weeks to find out who was going to be president. Bush won by five electoral votes, but his opponent, Al Gore, won the popular vote by over 500,000. Gore conceded the election to Bush on December 13, 2000.

Crawford Ranch

NYFD

"DUBYA"

BARACK HUSSEIN OBAMA JR.

August 4, 1961 (Honolulu, Hawaii) **Born**
Democratic **Party**
Joseph Biden **Vice president**
6 feet 1 inch tall, 180 pounds **Physical**
WIFE **Michelle** DAUGHTERS **Sasha and Malia** Family

PRESIDENT **44**

2008-present

---

http://www.obamaspacebooktube.com

obamaspacebooktube.com

Browse People | Log In | Sign up

✪ PERSONAL ✪

Obama's parents divorced when he was only two years old. He was raised by his mother and his maternal grandmother. He studied law at Harvard and was the first African American president of the prestigious Harvard Law Review. Obama loves basketball, trail mix, The Godfather movies and spending time with his family.

✪ PRESIDENTIAL FIRSTS ✪

First African American elected to the office of president

★
Grammy Winner
Barack Obama has won two Grammy awards. Both Grammys were awarded for the audio book versions of his works, "The Audacity of Hope." and "Dreams From My Father."

Contacting Barack Obama

President Barack Obama is the first President to use the full power of the Internet during his campaign in 2008. He used Myspace, YouTube, Digg, Twitter, Linkedin, and Flickr as different ways to reach potential voters. In the end Obama raised millions of dollars from hundreds of thousands of people through the internet.

★
Favorite Food
President Obama loves to cook chili and eat pizza from a small pizzeria in Chicago.

CHANGE
THAT WORKS FOR YOU
WWW.BARACKOBAMA.COM

Washington   J. Adams   Jefferson   Madison

Monroe   J. Q. Adams   Jackson   Van Buren

W. Harrison   Tyler   Polk   Taylor

Fillmore   Pierce   Buchanan   Lincoln

A. Johnson   Grant   Hayes   Garfield

Arthur

Cleveland

B. Harrison

McKinley

T. Roosevelt

Taft

Wilson

Harding

Coolidge

Hoover

F. Roosevelt

Truman

Eisenhower

Kennedy

L. Johnson

Nixon

Ford

Carter

Reagan

Bush

Clinton

Bush

Obama

WHAT DOES A PRESIDENT DO?

The president acts both as a political leader and as a symbol of our nation. He or she is the "Chief Executive" in charge of enforcing the laws of the country and running the executive branch of the government. He or she is Commander in Chief of the military. The president works with the Senate and the House of Representatives. He or she negotiates treaties with other countries and appoints judges, ambassadors, and other high government officials. The president can veto legislation proposed by Congress, while it takes the approval of the president and the entire Congress to pass legislation. (A veto may be overridden if the Senate and the House of Representatives both vote with a two-thirds majority.)

The Constitution outlines five areas that make up the president's job description:

1. Commander In Chief

The president is in charge of the military forces (the Army, Navy, Air Force, and Marines). The Constitution was designed so that the president and Congress must share the responsibility of declaring war, but in case of emergency the president may send troops without congressional approval.

2. Chief Administrator

The president is in charge of appointing people to fill government jobs.

3. Chief Diplomat

The president is the country's representative to the rest of the world. The president can make treaties (with the Senate's approval), nominate diplomats (if the Senate approves), and host visitors from other countries.

4. Chief Legislator

The president is in charge of giving Congress a list of items that are important and timely. Congress must discuss and propose action for each of these items. If the president doesn't like the result of Congress' vote, he or she can vote against it by using a veto.

5. Chief Magistrate

The president is in charge of seeing that the laws of the United States are followed and obeyed.

Learn more about presidential responsibilities at www.prezquest.com.

PREZQUEST
5
.COM

Tommy awoke
in a puddle of drool.
He had fallen asleep
preparing for school.
He looked at their work,
they broke into smiles—
history gave them the
THE TUPPERMAN FILES.

Tommy burst out the door,
he couldn't be late.
Today was the day
of the giant debate.

Penelope chose to give her speech first.
She said, "I am the best and he is the worst!
I promise you everything under the sun.
I am the **one** that represents fun."

(On the other hand...)

Tommy's speech would've
made Honest Abe proud.
He stood smart and tall
as he talked to the crowd.
He spoke of the truth
and responsible acts,
To vote with your brain
and consider the facts.
He stuck out his chest and said,

"I'm no **slob**—I am the one
who will do the best **job**!"

The votes were all counted with the greatest of care,
And the time had arrived to finally declare:

A winner.

Mrs. Snodgrass opened a very small note
That had written on it the results of the vote.
She read it aloud as the students sat frozen.
It was, yes indeed, Tommy they'd chosen.

Tommy was hit by a **fuzzy** sensation, as the crowd gave him a standing ovation.
He noticed, however, while hearing the cheers, that smoke poured out of Penelope's ears.
She started to slobber and her eyes turned dark red,
She yelled, "Tommy Tupperman,

I'll step on your head!"

Mrs. Snodgrass grabbed
Penelope by the scruff of the neck,
and told the young lady
she might want to check
her schedule for things
that might interfere . . .

. . . with the detention she'll have
for the rest of the **year.**

So...

If you happen to visit Rhino Grade School,
You might want to consider one very big rule:

Whenever you leave in the middle of class,
You better have with you an official hall pass,
Because any attempt to walk down the hall
Is watched by the tops, the best of them all—

and

★ Tommy **Tupperman's** ★

his name!

All secure in the hall!

Ray Nelson is a great big guy. (He's six feet four inches tall and weighs too much.) Most people look at Ray and think he should be a professional wrestler. Ray's favorite president is George Washington because he wore a wig and was still cool enough to be president. Ray hopes to someday build a vacation home out of Lincoln Logs. Ray spends most of his time hanging out in Portland, Oregon, with his wife, Theresa and their three children, Allie, Zach and Chase.

Douglas Kelly is a very small man. He lives in a renovated Malibu Barbie playhouse in Ray's garage. He enjoys jazz, golf, and painting. Doug's favorite president is the guy on the twenty dollar bill. (This is the biggest bill Doug has ever seen. Otherwise we guess he would probably like the guy on the thousand dollar bill.)

Ben Adams is a simple man with simple needs. Give Ben heavy metal music, a comic book, and some animal crackers, and he is as content as can be. Ben sports long brown hair and tiny little round glasses. Ben's favorite president is Benjamin Franklin. (Good thing Ben didn't write the educational information for this book.)

Mike McLane's favorite president is William Taft. Mike thinks a president should have sturdy thighs and a hardy appetite—traits for which Taft was notable. Mike lives in Bend, Oregon, with his wife, Holly, and their three children.

HISTORICAL CONSULTANTS

Keith Melder is *curator emeritus* at the National Museum of American History, Smithsonian Institution. Keith is the author of *Hail to the Candidate*, a book about presidential elections.

M.W. Pete Smith has been a history teacher for 40 years. He is an expert on U.S. presidents and a collector of presidential campaign buttons.

The George W. Bush and Barack Obama pages were added after Mr. Melder and Mr. Smith's involvement with this project.

SPECIAL THANKS

President Gerald Ford, Penny Circle, Bruce Barnet, Bob Savage, Sydney & Shine Thomas, Tim Weakland, Mark Watson, Jessi Wyse, Nate Scott, Kyle Holveck, Sarah Fong, Theresa Nelson Bill and Vicky Meyer, Jim Wilson, Julie Hanson, Chris Nelson, Jen Cleary, Kelly Kuntz, Ray Nelson Sr., Joseph Siegel, and Janet Lockwood.